Speak in a Week™
Spanish
Week Two

Designed by Donald S.
Illustrated by Julie Bra

Produced & distribut

Penton Overseas, Inc.
Carlsbad, CA

Speak in a Week®
Spanish:
Week Two

Published and distributed by Penton Overseas, Inc.,
1958 Kellogg Ave., Carlsbad, CA 92008.
www.pentonoverseas.com

Contact publisher by phone at (800) 748-5804
or via email, info@pentonoverseas.com.

ISBN 1-59125-286-5

Contents:

How to Use Speak in a Week:

Start with **Lesson Nine.** If you've studied Spanish before, you'll move on more quickly. Follow the lessons in order so you learn everything well. Master each lesson before you go to the next one.

Each lesson begins with an outline of what you'll be learning, followed by ten illustrated examples, first in Spanish, then in English. For every lesson, there's a track on the audio CD to help you with Spanish pronunciation.

On the illustrated pages, you'll also find extra grammar tips, helpful hints, and interesting facts about Spanish-speaking cultures. Following the eight lessons, you'll find a reference section with basic info, more words, and extra grammar.

When you've finished the lessons, go to the audio CD and listen to the last five tracks: **The Mastery Exercises.** You'll play with the Spanish you now know, so that you'll be able to make new sentences from what you've learned.

You'll be speaking Spanish!

Lesson 9

In this lesson you will learn...

- to ask questions using the words, *What?, Where?, When?, Who?, Why?, Which?, How?,* etc.

☞ **¿Qué?, ¿Dónde?, ¿Cuándo?, ¿Quién?, ¿Por qué?, ¿Cuál?, ¿Cómo?, etc.**

- some common "question" phrases.

☞ **¿Qué hora es?, ¿Dónde trabaja?, ¿Cuál quiere?, ¿Quién es?, etc...**

In Spanish, there are nine important "question" words that are absolutely essential to know. Learn the words below and you'll be able to request information about anyone or anything:

¿Qué?	**What?**
¿Dónde?	**Where?**
¿Cuándo?	**When?**
¿Cuánto?	**How much?**
¿Cuántos?	**How many?**
¿Quién?	**Who?**
¿Por qué?	**Why?**
¿Cuál?	**Which/What?**
¿Cómo?	**How?**

Note: All question words in Spanish have an accent mark. There is also an inverted question mark (¿) at the beginning of the question.

Que (without an accent) can mean that or than: Él es mayor que yo. (He's older than me.) - El carro que me gusta. (The car that I like.)

3

Glossary pg. 234 presents other What? & How? questions to practice.

4

¿Qué hora es?
*keh **oh**-rah-ehs*

For hours between 1:00 and 1:59, use es: Es la una. (It's 1:00.) All other hours are plural and use son: Son las dos. (It's 2:00.)

What time is it?

Learn to express time
easily by memorizing
the chart on Glossary pg.
184, What Time Is It?

¿Dónde trabaja?
dohn-deh trah-bah-hah

¿Adónde? (to where) is used to ask where someone or something is going. ¿Adónde va? - Where are you going (to)?

7

Practice more useful Where? & When? questions on Glossary pgs. 231-232.

Another way to ask how much something costs is to say: ¿Cuánto es? (How much is it?)

Practice asking How Much? & How Many? on Glossary pg. 236.

¿Cuántos? is used to ask How many? When you are referring to a feminine noun, it becomes ¿Cuántas?

Need a bag, bucket or basket? Pick one of the Containers on Glossary pg. 205.

If there is more than one who, say: ¿Quiénes son?
(Who are they? or Who are you (plural)?)

13

Learn the question words well. You'll see them again in Lesson 16 as you begin to form more complex sentences.

Try not to confuse **¿Por qué?**, with porque (because).
Porque (because) has no accent and is written as one word.

15

Try learning some of the Common Phrases on Glossary pgs. 229-230. Add a few to your conversations and you'll sound very fluent!

¿Cómo puedo ayudarle?

koh-moh *pweh*-doh *ah-yoo*-**dahr**-*leh*

If you didn't hear what a person said, the polite way of saying What? is ¿Cómo? (Not ¿Qué?)

How can I help you?

Watch out! Como, without an accent, can mean like, as, or even I eat.

18

If you want to ask what time the train arrives, say: ¿Cuándo llega el tren? (When does the train arrive?)

For a list of common When? questions, see Glossary pg. 232.

20

To ask about more than one (Which ones?), say: ¿Cuáles? Watch out! ¿Cuál? is often used to express What?

Which one do you want?

The What? & Which? questions on Glossary pg. 235 make up some of the most common expressions you will need to know.

Lesson 10

In this lesson you will learn...

- to talk about <u>activities</u> you *like* and *dislike*
  - ☞ **Me gusta, ¿Le gusta?, No me gusta**

- to talk about <u>activities</u> you *would like* to do
  - ☞ **Me gustaría, ¿Le gustaría?**

- to talk about actions
  - ☞ **hablar, escuchar, trabajar, leer, jugar, comprar, hacer, etc.**

Lessons 10 through 15 will teach you to talk about *actions* people do every day, such as walk, talk, eat, play, etc. All of the actions (verbs) are presented in their infinitive form. For example: **hablar** *(to speak)*, **comer** *(to eat)*, **escribir** *(to write)*.

Pay special attention to how the language concepts in lessons 10 through 15 are divided into small blocks of words or phrases, each independent of the other. The words in the upper left hand corner, the upper right hand corner, and those below the pictures, can all be moved between the lessons to form new and different sentences, using the same group of language concepts.

As your knowledge of the language increases, practice changing the different blocks, mixing and matching them to create new sentences of your own.

Me gusta...
*meh **goos**-tah*

hablar
*ah-**blahr***

con mis amigos.
*kohn mees ah-**mee**-gohs*

Hablar **can also mean** to speak.
Me gusta hablar español. (I like to speak Spanish.)

25

I like... to talk

with my friends.

Study the different blocks of text on each page as separate concepts, then practice putting them together as a whole.

Me gusta...
meh goos-tah

viajar
beeah-hahr

en agosto.
ehn ah-gohs-toh

Change what you want to say by substituting one word for another. Me gusta viajar con mis amigos. (I like to travel with my friends.)

I like... to travel

in August.

Learn the Months of the Year (Glossary pg. 184)
with the exercises in this lesson.

28

No me gusta...
*noh meh **goos**-tah*

trabajar
*trah-bah-**hahr***

los sábados.
*lohs **sah**-bah-dohs*

To express **on** Saturday, say: **el sábado** (singular).
To express **on** Saturdays, say: **los sábados** (plural).

I don't like... to work

on Saturdays.

Make sure you know how to say on Monday, on Tuesday, etc. by studying all the Days of the Week on Glossary pg. 183.

¿Le gusta...
leh goos-tah

leer
leh-ehr

libros románticos?
lee-brohs roh-mahn-tee-kohs

If you want to say, I like to read romantic books, just substitute Me gusta... for ¿Le gusta...? – Me gusta leer libros románticos.

Do you like... to read

romantic books?

Don't forget! Adjectives of quality follow the noun, and must agree in number and gender with the noun they modify.

¿Le gusta...
*leh **goos**-tah*

jugar
*hoo-**gahr***

al golf?
ahl gohlf

Jugar **means** to play a sport. Tocar **means** to play a musical instrument. Me gusta tocar el piano. (I like to play the piano.)

33

Do you like...   to play

golf?

If you prefer to play a different kind of game, take your pick
from the list of Games & Toys on Glossary pg. 223.

Me gustaría...
*me goos-tah-**ree**-ah*

comprar
*kohm-**prahr***

una camisa nueva.
*oo-nah kah-**mee**-sah **nweh**-vah*

Another way of saying I would like... is Quisiera... (kee-**syeh**-rah).

I would like... to buy

a new shirt.

A popular four-pocket shirt called a chacavana is worn by men throughout Latin America.

Me gustaría...
*me goos-tah-**ree**-ah*

hacer
*ah-**sehr***

reservaciones.
*reh-sehr-vah-**syoh**-nehs*

Hacer can also mean to do. Me gustaría hacerlo hoy.
– I would like to do it today.

I would like... to make

reservations.

All verbs (in the infinitive form) end in either -ar, -er, or -ir. You'll see why this is good to know when you get to Lesson 20 in Week Three.

Me gustaría...
*meh goos-tah-**ree**-ah*

comer
*koh-**mehr***

a las siete.
*ah lahs **syeh**-teh*

Me gustaría comer is very different from Me gusta comer.
Me gustaría... is a more polite way of saying I want...

39

I would like... to eat

at seven o'clock.

In Latin America, la cena (dinner) is usually eaten after 8:00 p.m. In Spain, it is often served after 10:00 p.m.!

¿Le gustaría...
*le goos-tah-**ree**-ah*

tomar
*toh-**mahr***

una taza de café?
*oo-nah **tah**-sah deh kah-**feh***

The verb tomar can also mean to take. Me gustaría tomar el tren. (I would like to take the train.)

Would you like... to have

a cup of coffee?

Another common action you'll need to know is beber (to drink).

¿Le gustaría...
*le goos-tah-**ree**-ah*

ver
vehr

una película?
*oo-nah peh-**lee**-koo-lah*

In Spanish, you can either ver (see) una película or you can mirar (watch) una película.

43

Would you like...   to see

a movie?

If you would rather see a video,
the Spanish word is un vídeo.

Lesson 11

In this lesson you will learn...

- the subject pronouns *I*, *you*, *he*, *she*, *they*, etc.

  ☞ **yo, tú, usted, ustedes, él, ella, ellos, ellas, etc.**

- the different forms of the verb *to need*

  ☞ **necesito, necesitas, necesita, necesitamos, necesitan**

- new words of action

  ☞ **estudiar, ir, lavar, traer, pagar, descansar, escribir, cambiar, etc.**

45

Before beginning this lesson,
study the Spanish subject pronouns below:

Singular		Plural	
yo	I	**nosotros**	we *(masc.)*
		nosotras	we *(fem.)*
tú	you *(informal)*	**vosotros***	you *(inf. masc.)*
		vosotras*	you *(inf. fem.)*
usted	you *(formal)*	**ustedes**	you *(formal)*
él	he	**ellos**	they *(masc.)*
ella	she	**ellas**	they *(fem.)*

* The plural form of *tú* (*vosotros, vosotras*) is rarely used in the
Spanish-speaking world, outside of Spain. Because of its limited
use, it will not be emphasized in this program.

Yo necesito...
*yoh neh-seh-**see**-toh*

estudiar
*ehs-too-**dyahr***

para el examen.
*pah-rah ehl ehk-**sah**-mehn*

To express *I need*, say either *Yo necesito* or simply *Necesito*. The verb form *Necesito* already implies the *Yo*.

I need... to study

for the exam.

For more things you might find In the Classroom, see Glossary pg. 222.

Yo necesito...
yoh neh-seh-see-toh

ir
eer

al supermercado.
ahl soo-pehr-mehr-kah-doh

Remember: When a (to) is used before the article el (the), they form the contraction al (to the).

I need... to go

to the supermarket.

Small grocery stores are still very popular in many Spanish-speaking countries. Visit all The Stores on Glossary pgs. 218-219.

50

Usted necesita...
*oos-**tehd** neh-seh-**see**-tah*

lavar
*lah-**vahr***

el carro.
*ehl **kah**-rroh*

To express You need..., say either: Usted necesita...
or simply Necesita. The verb form Necesita already
implies the Usted.

You need... to wash

the car.

You can find all the cleaning supplies you need for the car, or the house, in The Laundry on Glossary pg. 210.

¿Necesita usted...
*neh-seh-**see**-tah oos-**tehd***

traer
*trah-**ehr***

tantas cosas?
***tahn**-tahs **koh**-sahs*

To ask a question using usted, you must reverse the word order. Remember: The word usted is frequently dropped.

53

Do you need... to bring

so many things?

Looks like this lady definitely needed un portero (a porter).
Hopefully, she will remember to give a tip (dar una propina).

Tú necesitas...
*too neh-seh-**see**-tahs*

pagar
*pah-**gahr***

la cuenta.
*lah **kwehn**-tah*

Tú is the familiar form of usted. Both mean you, but tú is used when speaking to friends and family (not strangers).

You need...
informal

to pay

the check.

Remember: The word informal below you means to
use the informal form for addressing someone.

Él necesita...
*ehl neh-seh-**see**-tah*

descansar
*dehs-kan-**sahr***

un poco.
*oon **poh**-koh*

Some words have an accent mark to clarify their meaning.
Él with an accent means he. El without an accent means the.

57

He needs... to rest

a little.

It is customary in most Spanish-speaking countries to take una siesta (a nap) during the middle of the day.

Ella necesita...
eh-yah neh-seh-see-tah

escribir
ehs-kree-beer

una carta.
oo-nah kahr-tah

Have you noticed? Él, ella, and usted all share the same form of to need. Él necesita... Ella necesita... and Usted necesita...

She needs... to write

a letter.

With help from The Post Office on Glossary pgs. 224-225, you'll find all the things you need to write and mail a letter successfully.

Ellos necesitan... cambiar
*eh-yohs neh-seh-**see**-tahn*   *kahm-**byahr***

cien dólares.
*syehn **doh**-lah-rehs*

The verb cambiar is commonly used to mean to change. Ellos necesitan cambiar de tren. (They need to change trains.)

They need...   to exchange

one hundred dollars.

If the they you are referring to are all females, use ellas. If they includes a mixed group of males and females, use ellos.

Ustedes necesitan...
*oos-**teh**-dehs neh-seh-**see**-tahn*

tomar
*toh-**mahr***

34 Barcelona
16 Madrid
12 Sevilla

el tren número doce.
*ehl trehn **noo**-meh-roh **doh**-seh*

Ustedes is the plural form of usted (you) and is used when referring to multiple people, as in "you guys."

63

You need...
plural

to take

34 Barcelona
16 Madrid
12 Sevilla

train number
twelve.

The plural below the word you means the sentence is
referring to multiple people, as in "you guys."

Nosotros necesitamos...   encontrar
*noh-**soh**-trohs neh-seh-see-**tah**-mohs*   *ehn-kohn-**trahr***

un banco.
*uhn **bahn**-koh*

Nosotros means we, but is often dropped when speaking as it is already implied by the verb form Necesitamos.

We need... to find

a bank.

Practice mixing and matching the vocabulary and concepts in Lessons 10 and 11 until you can combine them easily.

Lesson 12

In this lesson you will learn...

- the different forms of the verb *to want*
  - ☞ **quiero, quieres, quiere, queremos, quieren**

- new words of action
  - ☞ **aprender, sacar, escuchar, venir, vender, enviar, nadar, mirar, tener, esperar**

Before beginning this lesson, study the different forms of
the verb *querer* (*to want*).

Singular		Plural	
Yo	quiero	*Nosotros* *Nosotras* } queremos	
Tú	quieres		
Usted *Él* *Ella* } quiere		*Ustedes* *Ellos* *Ellas* } quieren	

Because Spanish verb endings indicate the subject of a sentence,
the subject pronouns are often dropped. In this lesson, you will
practice applying this concept to the verb *querer* (*to want*).

Quiero...
kyeh-roh

aprender
*ah-pren-**dehr***

español.
*ehs-pah-**nyohl***

The personal pronoun Yo (I) is often dropped in conversations as it is already implied in the verb form Quiero (I want).

I want... to learn

Spanish.

In Spanish, nationalities and languages are not capitalized unless they appear at the beginning of a sentence.

No quiero...
noh qyeh-roh

sacar
sah-cahr

la basura.
lah bah-soo-rah

Try not to confuse the verb sacar (to take out) with the verb quitar (to take off).

I don't want... to take out

the trash.

Once you take out the trash, why not fix those little things around the house with Tools & Materials on Glossary pgs. 212-213.

72

¿Quiere...
kyeh-reh

escuchar
*es-koo-**chahr***

música?
moo-see-kah

Literally translated, escuchar means to listen to.
The preposition a (to) is already included in the verb.

73

Do you want... to listen (to)

music?

Study Tip: Listen to Spanish radio stations. It will help you develop an ear for the rhythm and intonation of the language.

Quieres...
kyeh-rehs

venir
veh-neer

a mi casa?
ah mee kah-sah

Practice using the informal form of you when speaking to a friend, relative, child, or pet.

Do you want...
informal

to come

to my house?

All the exercises in this lesson express the idea of to want for different people without using the subject pronouns (Yo, Tú, etc.)

Tomás quiere...
*toh-**mahs** **kyeh**-reh*

vender
*vehn-**dehr***

su barco.
*soo **bahr**-koh*

Mastery Exercise: Tomás necesita vender su carro.

Thomas wants... to sell

his boat.

Lorena quiere...
loh-reh-nah kyeh-reh

enviar
ehn-vee-ahr

un paquete a su madre.
oon pah-keh-teh ah soo mah-dreh

Another word for enviar (to send) is mandar.

Lorena wants... to send

a package to her mother.

Each exercise contains multiple language concepts.
It's best to master each part of the exercise separately.

Quieren...
kyeh-rehn

nadar
nah-dahr

en la piscina.
ehn lah pee-see-nah

Notice how ellos (they) is not stated. That's because it's implied in the verb quieren.

They want... to swim

in the pool.

Have you started to see how you can substitute a word or group of words from another exercise, and say something totally different?

¿Quieren...
kyeh-rehn

mirar
mee-rahr

la televisión?
lah teh-leh-vee-syohn

La televisión refers to a program on the television.
The actual set is called el televisor.

Do you want...
plural
to watch

television?

Remember: The plural below the word you means the sentence is referring to multiple people, as in "you guys."

Queremos...
*keh-**reh**-mohs*

tener
*teh-**nehr***

una fiesta.
***oo**-nah **fyehs**-stah*

You've already seen Tengo (I have) and ¿Tiene? (Do you have?). They both come from the verb tener (to have).

We want...   to have

a party.

A young girl's fifteenth birthday celebration, una quinceañera, is an important event marking her transition into womanhood.

No queremos...
*noh keh-**reh**-mohs*

esperar
*ehs-peh-**rahr***

hasta mañana.
***ahs**-tah mah-**nyah**-nah*

Remember: To express the negative just put no in front of whatever you are saying!

We don't want...   to wait

until tomorrow.

It is essential to be able to express different Time Elements. Use Glossary pgs. 187-190 to learn how to say before, after, etc.

Lesson 13

In this lesson you will learn...

- to talk about activities you and other people *have to* do

☞ **Yo tengo que**
Tú tienes que
Usted tiene que, etc.

- new words of action

☞ **llamar, obtener, preguntar, hacer, regresar, limpiar, cortar, alquilar, partir, dejar**

You already know a couple of the forms of the verb *tener* (*to have*). Here are a few more:

Singular		Plural	
Yo	tengo	*Nosotros* *Nosotras* } tenemos	
Tú	tienes		
Usted *Él* *Ella* } tiene		*Ustedes* *Ellos* *Ellas* } tienen	

Note: When *que* is used after the different forms of the verb *tener*, it implies an *obligation* to do something. For example:
Tengo *el carro.* (**I have** *the car.*)
Tengo que *lavar el carro.* (**I have to** *wash the car.*)

Tengo que...
tehn-goh keh

obtener
ohb-teh-nehr

una visa.
oo-nah vee-sah

Use Tengo with people and things: Tengo una visa. Use Tengo que with actions: Tengo que obtener una visa.

I have... to get

a visa.

Get ready for Trips & Travel with Glossary pgs. 214-215.
While you're there, check In the Hotel with
Glossary pgs. 218-219.

Tengo que...
tehn-goh keh

llamar
*yah-**mahr***

a mi esposa.
*a mee ehs-**poh**-sah*

The word "a" is used with verbs when referring to people. See Glossary pg. 237 for an explanation of the Personal A.

I have... to call

my wife.

Don't forget to refer to Glossary pgs. 191-192 and learn the Family Members. If you don't yet know them, now is the time!

Tienes que...
tyeh-nehs keh

preguntar
preh-goon-tahr

a tu madre.
*ah too **mah**-dreh*

In Lesson 6 of Week One, you learned to express your as su or sus. In the informal form, your becomes tu or tus.

95

You have...
informal

to ask

your mother.

Make sure you look at Glossary pg. 237 for an explanation of the Personal A.

¿Tienes que...
tyeh-nehs-keh

hacer
*ah-**sehr***

tu tarea?
*too tah-**reh**-ah*

Remember: The verb hacer can also be used to express to make (hacer reservaciones - to make reservations).

Do you have...

informal

to do

your homework?

Study Tip: Take this book with you everwhere! Study when you're waiting in line, on a break, during a commercial, etc.

Ud. tiene que...
*oos-**tehd** **tyeh**-neh keh*

regresar
*reh-greh-**sahr***

más tarde.
*mahs **tahr**-deh*

Ud. is the abbreviation for usted.
A synonym of regresar is volver.

You have...   to return

later.

Another way to say to return is volver. To return something (such as books), use devolver.

Ella tiene que...
eh-yah *tyeh*-neh keh

limpiar
leem-**pyahr**

la sala.
lah **sah**-*lah*

Mastery Exercise: Él tiene que limpiar la cocina.

She has...   to clean

the living room.

Mastery Exercise: He has to clean the kitchen.

Él tiene que...
ehl tyeh-neh keh

cortar
kohr-tahr

el césped.
ehl sehs-pehd

Other names for grass include la grama, el pasto, and la hierba. Hierba is also the word for herb. A mala hierba is a weed.

He has... to cut

the grass.

There are many words to describe other things you'll find Inside & Outside the house. Look them up on Glossary pg. 207.

Uds. tienen que...
*oos-**teh**-dehs **tyeh**-nehn keh*

dejar
*deh-**hahr***

una propina.
*oo-nah proh-**pee**-nah*

Uds. is the abbreviation for ustedes.

You have...
plural

to leave

a tip.

Some restaurants include the tip in the bill. Look at la cuenta. It will read: servicio incluido (service included).

Ellos tienen que...
eh-yohs tyeh-nehn keh

partir
pahr-teer

el ocho de abril.
ehl oh-choh deh ah-breel

When expressing the date in Spanish, the number comes before the month.

They have... to leave

April 8th.

Glossary pg. 185 will give you help expressing
Dates & Large Numbers.

Tenemos que...
*teh-**neh**-mohs keh*

alquilar
*ahl-kee-**lahr***

un apartamento.
*oon ah-pahr-tah-**mehn**-toh*

Mastery Exercise: Queremos alquilar unas bicicletas.

We have... to rent

an apartment.

Mastery Exercise: We want to rent some bicycles.

Lesson 14

In this lesson you will learn...

- to talk about activities you and other people are *going to* do

☛ **Yo voy a**
Tú vas a
Usted va a, etc.

- new words of action

☛ **apagar, dormir, visitar, llegar, llevar, ayudar, correr, terminar, buscar, pasar**

In this lesson you will learn to use the verb *ir* (*to go*) to express actions you and other people are *going to* do in the future.

Singular		Plural	
Yo	voy	*Nosotros* }vamos *Nosotras*	
Tú	vas		
Usted *Él* }va *Ella*		*Ustedes* *Ellos* }van *Ellas*	

Note: Say the word "*a*" after the above forms to express an action you are *going to* do.

*Voy **a** lavar el carro.* (*I'm going to wash the car.*)

Voy a...
voy ah

apagar
ah-pah-gahr

la luz.
lah loos

If you're going to turn on the light, say: Voy a prender la luz.

I am going to... turn off

the light.

If you turn the light on and it doesn't work, you probably need to change the light bulb (cambiar el foco).

¿Vas a...
vahs ah

dormir
dohr-meer

todo el día?
toh-doh ehl dee-ah

Mastery Exercise: ¿Vas a trabajar todo el día?

Are you going to...   sleep

informal

all day?

Mastery Exercise: Are you going to work all day?

¿Va Ud. a...

*vah oos-**tehd** ah*

visitar

*vee-see-**tahr***

la catedral?

*lah kah-teh-**drahl***

Remember: Saying usted is optional.
(¿Va a visitar la catedral?)

·117

Are you going to... visit

the cathedral?

If you like to go sightseeing, be sure to stop by the Points of Interest on Glossary pg. 227.

Él va a...
ehl vah ah

llegar
*yeh-**gahr***

tarde.
tahr-deh

Mastery Exercise: Ella va a llegar a las seis y media.

He is going to... arrive

late.

Mastery Exercise: She's going to arrive at six-thirty.
Need help? Review What Time Is It?, Glossary pg. 186.

Ella va a...
eh-yah vah ah

llevar
*yeh-**vahr***

su sombrero favorito.
*soo sohm-**breh**-roh fah-voh-**ree**-toh*

The verb llevar can also mean to carry as in: Ella va a llevar a su hijo a casa. (She is going to take [carry] her son home.)

She is going to... wear

her favorite hat.

Study the Clothing & Jewelry items on Glossary pgs. 193-196 and you'll be able to talk about everything you are going to wear.

Carlitos va a...
*kahr-**lee**-tohs vah ah*

ayudar
*ah-yoo-**dahr***

a su tía.
*ah soo **tee-ah***

The verb ayudar is followed by a when referring to a person.
See Glossary pg. 237 for use of the Personal A.

Carlitos is going to...   help

his aunt.

The endings -ito, -ita, -itos, and -itas are often added to the end of a name as a sign of endearment, or to show smallness in size.

Ellos van a...
eh-yohs vahn ah

correr
*koh-**rrehr***

cinco kilómetros
***seen**-koh kee-**loh**-meh-trohs*

Remember: If the they to whom you are referring are all females, you would use ellas.

They are going to...   run

five kilometers.

A kilometer is approximately 3/5 of una milla (a mile).
See weights and measurements on Glossary pg. 240.

¿Van a...
vahn ah

terminar
*tehr-mee-**nahr***

hoy?
oy

Ustedes is already implied in the verb form van. If speaking
to only one person, you would ask: ¿Va a terminar hoy?

Are you going to... *plural* finish

today?

Another way to say to finish is acabar.

128

Vamos a...
vah-mohs ah

pasar
*pah-**sahr***

muchos puntos de interés
*moo-chohs **poon**-tohs deh een-teh-**rehs***

Pasar also means to happen or to spend (time). ¿Cómo va a pasar el día? (How are you going to spend the day?)

We are going to... pass

many points
of interest.

In many Spanish-speaking countries, it is very common to
dar un paseo (take a walk) in the early evening.

Vamos a...
vah-mohs ah

buscar
boos-kahr

unos recuerdos.
oo-nohs reh-kwehr-dohs

If you just want to say Let's go!, as in "we're leaving," say: Vámonos!

Let's go... look for

some souvenirs.

Una tienda de regalos (a gift shop) will generally have a good selection of souveniers and gifts for everyone.

Lesson 15

In this lesson you will learn...

- to talk about activities you and other people *can* (*are able*) to do
- **Yo puedo, Tú puedes, Él puede, Ella puede, Ellos pueden, etc.**

- new words of action
- **tocar, usar, recordar, abrir, dar, manejar, cocinar, caminar, bailar, estacionar**

In this lesson you will learn to use the verb *poder* (*to be able*) to express actions that you and other people *can* or *can't* do:

Singular		Plural	
Yo	puedo	*Nosotros* *Nosotras* }	podemos
Tú	puedes		
Usted *Él* *Ella* }	puede	*Ustedes* *Ellos* *Ellas* }	pueden

Note: The actions in the upper right hand corner on the English pgs. in this lesson are written without the "*to*" which normally accompanies the infinitive verb. The "*to*" is implied but has been omitted for it to make sense in English.

Yo puedo...
*yoh **pweh**-doh*

tocar
*toh-**kahr***

el piano.
*ehl **pyah**-noh*

The verb tocar means to touch or to play a musical instrument. The verb jugar (to play) is used if referring to a sport or game.

135

I can...   play

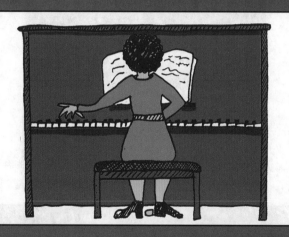

the piano.

Don't forget to use tracks 1-8 on the CD to practice
each lesson and help with your pronunciation.

¿Puedo...
pweh-doh

usar
oo-sahr

el teléfono?
ehl teh-leh-foh-noh

Mastery Exercise: ¿Puedo apagar la luz?

Can I...   use

the telephone?

Mastery Exercise: Can I turn off the light?

No puedo...
*noh **pweh**-doh*

abrir
*ah-**breer***

la puerta
*lah **pwehr**-tah*

The opposite of abrir is cerrar (seh-rrahr), which means to close.

I can't... open

the door.

If you're really stuck and can't get out, yell: ¡Soccoro! (Help!).
For more Survival Phrases, see Glossary pg. 228.

No puedo...
*noh **pweh**-doh*

recordar
*reh-kohr-**dahr***

el número.
*ehl **noo**-meh-roh*

Mastery Exercise: No puedo hacer eso.

I can't... remember

the number.

Mastery Exercise: I can't do that. To express
This & That, see Glossary pgs. 238-239.

142

¿Puede...
pweh-deh

dar
dahr

esto a la recepcionista?

ehs-toh ah lah
reh-sehp-syoh-**nee**-stah

If you want to say these instead of this, use estos.

Can you...   give

this to the
receptionist?

Be sure to look over Glossary pgs. 238-239 for
the rules on This & That. They are used frequently,
and are important to know.

¿Puedes...
pweh-dehs

manejar
*mah-neh-**hahr***

más despacio
por favor?
*mahs dehs-**pah**-syoh pohr-fah-**vohr***

If you prefer to go faster, say: Más rápido, por favor!

Can you... *informal*

drive

slower please?

Another way to say *to drive* is conducir (kohn-doo-seer).

Carlos no puede...
*kahr-lohs noh **pweh**-deh*

cocinar
*koh-see-**nahr***

muy bien.
mwee byehn

Mastery Exercise: A él no le gusta cocinar.

Carlos can't...   cook

very well.

Mastery Exercise: He doesn't like to cook.

Ellos pueden...
eh-yohs pweh-dehn

bailar
bah-ee-lahr

la salsa.
lah sahl-sah

La salsa is a popular Latin American dance (and music) of Afro-Cuban origin.

They can... dance

the salsa.

Other dances you'll want to get lessons on include
el merengue, la cumbia, **and** el chachachá.

¿Pueden..
pweh-dehn

caminar
*kah-mee-**nahr***

más rápido?
*mahs **rah**-pee-doh*

Mastery Exercise: Tenemos que caminar más rápido.

Can you...
plural

walk

faster?

Mastery Exercise: We have to walk faster.

Podemos...
*poh-**deh**-mohs*

estacionar
*ehs-tah-syoh-**nahr***

aquí.
*ah-**kee***

Anytime you give or receive directions, you'll need these words: ahí, allí (there), allá (there, over there), aquí, acá (here).

153

We can... park

here.

Take some time to review Lessons 9-14
before moving on to Lesson 16.

Lesson 16

In this lesson you will...

- review the question words

  ☞ **¿Qué?, ¿Dónde?, ¿Cuándo?, ¿Quién?, ¿Por qué?, etc.**

- practice making questions out of words and concepts from this lesson

  ☞ **¿Qué quieres jugar? ¿Cómo vas a pagar? ¿Cuál quiere comprar?, etc.**

Once you can use the concepts from this lesson, you will be well on your way to becoming a master at speaking Spanish. You still, however, need to review what you have learned so far.

Upon completion of Lesson 16, make sure you use the Mastery Exercises on the CD (tracks 9-13) to practice mixing and matching the words and phrases from the previous lessons. If you are confident in your ability to understand and recall the words quickly, move on to Lesson 17 in Week Three. But, remember! The only one who can judge your mastery is you. Be honest with yourself and concentrate on building a strong foundation. If you need some help in a few areas, go back and review.

Note: The phonetic guides are not in this lesson since you have already seen most of the words before. From now on, the phonetic guides will only appear under words of unusual difficulty.

¿Qué quieres jugar?

What **do you want** to play?
informal

Mastery Exercise: What are you (informal) going to do?

¿Qué le gustaría tomar?

Mastery Exercise: ¿Qué quiere comer?

What **would** you like to drink?

Mastery Exercise: What do you want to eat?

¿Cuándo necesita regresar?

When do you need to return?

Mastery Exercise: When are you (informal) going to study?

¿Dónde puedo encontrar un taxi?

Mastery Exercise: ¿Dónde puedo estacionar?

Where can I find a taxi?

Mastery Exercise: Where can I park?

¿Cuánto quiere cambiar?

Mastery Exercise: ¿Cuánto necesitamos?

165

How much do you want to exchange?

Mastery Exercise: How much do we need?

166

¿Cuántos puedes ver?

Mastery Exercise: ¿Cuántos kilómetros van a correr?

How many can you see?
informal

Mastery Exercise: How many kilometers are they going to run?

¿Por qué no le gusta bailar?

Mastery Exercise: ¿Por qué tengo que sacar la basura?

Why don't you like to dance?

Mastery Exercise: Why do I have to take out the trash?

¿Cómo vas a pagar?

Mastery Exercise: ¿Cómo vamos a enviar el paquete?

How are you going to pay?

informal

Mastery Exercise: How are we going to send the package?

¿Quién necesita ir al baño?

Mastery Exercise: ¿Quién quiere mirar la televisión?

Who needs to go to the bathroom?

¿Cuál quiere comprar?

Mastery Exercise: ¿Cuál le gusta?

175

Which one do you want to buy?

Glossary

Glossary (cntd.)

Spanish Alphabet

a	ah	**n**	**eh**-neh
b	beh	**ñ**	**ehn**-yeh
c	seh	**o**	oh
ch	cheh	**p**	peh
d	deh	**q**	koo
e	eh	**r**	**eh**-reh
f	**eh**-feh	**rr**	**eh**-rreh
g	heh	**s**	**eh**-seh
h	**ah**-cheh	**t**	teh
i	ee	**u**	oo
j	**hoh**-tah	**v**	veh
k	kah	**w**	**doh**-bleh veh
l	**eh**-leh	**x**	**eh**-kees
ll	**eh**-yeh	**y**	ee-gree-**eh**-gah
m	**eh**-meh	**z**	**seh**-tah

The Spanish alphabet contains four letters that are not found in English: **ch**, **ll**, **ñ**, and **rr**.

Spanish Vowels

These are the most important sounds in Spanish
and they will almost always sound the same.

Vowel		**Sounds like the...**	**Spanish Word**
a	**(ah)**	**a** as in f**a**ther	casa *(**kah**-sah)*
e	**(eh)**	**e** as in b**e**d, l**e**t	mesa *(**meh**-sah)*
i	**(ee)**	**ee** as in m**ee**t, f**ee**t	libro *(**lee**-broh)*
o	**(oh)**	**o** in **o**ld, **o**kay	hotel *(oh-**tehl**)*
u	**(oo)**	**oo** in m**oo**n, s**oo**n	lunes *(**loo**-nehs)*

Sometimes two or more letters come together and make another
sound. Don't worry! You'll learn those sounds as they appear!

Sounds of Spanish

c   Before **a**, **o**, **u**, or a **consonant**, like the **k** in *kite*.
Before **e** or **i**, like the **s** in *see*.

cc   Always sounds like the **x** in *tax*.

ch   Like the **ch** in *church*.

d   Usually like the **d** in *dog*. Between vowels or at the end of a syllable, **d** sounds like **th**, as in *that*.

g   Before **a**, **o**, or **u**, hard, like the **g** in *go*.
Before **e** or **i**, soft, like the **h** in *hat*.

h   The Spanish **h** is **always silent!**

j   Like the **h** in *hat*.

Sounds of Spanish

l   If only one **l**, it sounds like the **l** in *leave*.

ll   The double **ll** sounds like the **y** in *yell*.

ñ   Sounds like the **ny** in *canyon*.

r   Slightly rolled or trilled.

rr   Heavily trilled.

v   A cross between **v** and **b**. It is pronounced like a very soft **v**, much like the **v** in *mauve*.

y   Like the **y** in *yet* **unless it appears alone,** then it sounds like the **ee** in *feet* and means **"*and*"**.

z   Always sounds like the **s** in *see*.

The letters **k** and **w** are used only to spell words from other languages, such as *kilo, ketchup, Washington*.

Days Of The Week

Days of the week and months of the year are not capitalized unless they appear at the beginning of a sentence. Notice the Spanish calendar (*el calendario*) begins on Monday.

Monday	el lunes	*ehl **loo**-nehs*
Tuesday	el martes	*ehl **mahr**-tehs*
Wednesday	el miércoles	*ehl **myehr**-koh-lehs*
Thursday	el jueves	*ehl **hweh**-behs*
Friday	el viernes	*ehl **vyehr**-nehs*
Saturday	el sábado	*ehl **sah**-bah-doh*
Sunday	el domingo	*ehl doh-**meen**-goh*

Spanish-speakers never use *en* (*on*), when expressing a certain day. Instead, they use the article *el* or *los*. For example:

*Salgo **el** lunes. (I'm leaving on Monday).*

Months Of The Year

January	enero	*eh-**neh**-roh*
February	febrero	*feh-**breh**-roh*
March	marzo	***mahr**-soh*
April	abril	*ah-**breel***
May	mayo	***mah**-yoh*
June	junio	***hoo**-neeoh*
July	julio	***hoo**-leeoh*
August	agosto	*ah-**gohs**-toh*
September	septiembre	*sehp-**tyehm**-breh*
October	octubre	*ohk-**too**-breh*
November	noviembre	*noh-**vyehm**-breh*
December	diciembre	*dee-**syehm**-breh*

Dates & Large Numbers

To express the specific date or time of an event, you simply use the days, months and large numbers you already know.

The year 1997 is expressed exactly like the number 1,997:
mil novecientos noventa y siete

To express the date July 4, 1963, you give:
the day + the month + the year
El cuatro de julio, mil novecientos sesenta y tres.

To give the date something began, say: ***Desde ...*** (*Since...*)
Desde mil novecientos cincuenta y tres (*Since 1953*)

To express the year you were born, use: ***Nací...*** (*I was born...*)
Nací en mil novecientos setenta. (*I was born in 1970.*)

What Time Is It?

What time is it?	*¿Qué hora es?*	----------
From 1:00 - 1:59:	*Es la una...*	*It's 1:00*
From 2:00 on:	*Son las dos...*	*It's 2:00*
Before the hour:	*Es la una menos veinte.*	*It's 12:40*
hour less minutes	*Son las dos menos cinco.*	*It's 1:55*
menos (less)	*Son las tres menos diez.*	*It's 2:50*
After the hour:	*Es la una y diez.*	*It's 1:10*
hour plus minutes	*Son las tres y cuarto.*	*It's 3:15*
using **y** *(and)*	*Son las dos y media.*	*It's 2:30*
Exactly the hour:	*Es exactamente la una.*	*1:00 exactly*
On the dot:	*Son las dos en punto.*	*2:00 sharp*
The half hour:	*Son las tres y media.*	*It's 3:30*

Time Elements

today	**hoy**	oy
in the morning	**en la mañana**	*ehn lah mah-**nyah**-nah*
in the afternoon	**en la tarde**	*ehn lah **tahr**-deh*
in the evening	**en la noche**	*ehn lah **noh**-cheh*
this morning	**esta mañana**	***ehs**-tah mah-**nyah**-nah*
this afternoon	**esta tarde**	***ehs**-tah **tahr**-deh*
tonight	**esta noche**	***ehs**-tah **noh**-cheh*
on the dot	**en punto**	*ehn **poon**-toh*
noon	**el mediodía**	*ehl meh-dyoh-**dee**-ah*
as soon as possible	**lo más pronto posible**	*loh mahs **prohn**-toh poh-**see**-bleh*

Time Elements (cntd.)

tomorrow	**mañana**	*mah-**nyah**-nah*
the day after tomorrow	**pasado mañana**	*pah-**sah**-doh mah-**nyah**-nah*
yesterday	**ayer**	*ah-**yehr***
the day before yesterday	**anteayer**	*ahn-teh-ah-**yehr***
last night	**anoche**	*ah-**noh**-cheh*
the week	**la semana**	*lah seh-**mah**-nah*
last week	**la semana pasada**	*...pah-**sah**-dah*
each week	**cada semana**	***kah**-dah...*
next week	**la próxima semana**	*lah **prohk**-see-ma...*
the weekend	**el fin de semana**	*ehl feen deh...*

Time Elements (cntd.)

a moment	**un momento**	*oon moh-**mehn**-toh*
after	**después (de)**	*dehs-**pwehs** deh*
all the time	**todo el tiempo**	*toh doh ehl **tyehm**-poh*
always	**siempre**	***syehm**-preh*
before	**antes**	***ahn**-tehs*
during	**durante**	*doo-**rahn**-teh*
early	**temprano**	*tehm-**prah**-noh*
everyday	**todos los días**	***toh**-dohs lohs **dee**-ahs*
late	**tarde**	***tahr**-deh*
later	**más tarde**	*mahs **tahr**-deh*
lots of times	**muchas veces**	***moo**-chahs **veh**-sehs*

Time Elements (cntd.)

never	**nunca**	*noon-kah*
now	**ahora**	*ah-oh-rah*
often	**a menudo**	*ah meh-noo-doh*
once	**una vez**	*oo-nah vehs*
right now	**ahorita**	*ah-oh-ree-tah*
seldom	**casi nunca**	*kah-see noon-kah*
since	**desde**	*dehs-deh*
sometimes	**a veces**	*ah veh-sehs*
soon	**pronto**	*prohn-toh*
still	**todavía**	*toh-dah-vee-ah*
lately, recently	**últimamente**	*oohl-tee-mah-mehn-teh*
until	**hasta**	*ahs-tah*

Family Members

father	**el padre**	*ehl **pah**-dreh*
mother	**la madre**	*lah **mah**-dreh*
son	**el hijo**	*ehl **ee**-hoh*
daughter	**la hija**	*lah **ee**-hah*
brother	**el hermano**	*ehl ehr-**mah**-noh*
sister	**la hermana**	*lah ehr-**mah**-nah*
grandfather	**el abuelo**	*ehl ah-**bweh**-loh*
grandmother	**la abuela**	*lah ah-**bweh**-lah*
grandson	**el nieto**	*ehl **nyeh**-toh*
granddaughter	**la nieta**	*lah **nyeh**-tah*
uncle	**el tío**	*ehl **tee**-oh*
aunt	**la tía**	*lah **tee**-ah*

Family Members (cntd.)

cousin (male)	**el primo**	*ehl **pree**-moh*
cousin (female)	**la prima**	*lah **pree**-mah*
nephew	**el sobrino**	*ehl soh-**bree**-noh*
niece	**la sobrina**	*lah soh-**bree**-nah*
baby	**el bebé**	*ehl beh-**beh***
small boy	**el niño**	*ehl **nee**-nyoh*
small girl	**la niña**	*lah **nee**-nyah*
young boy	**el muchacho**	*ehl moo-**chah**-choh*
young girl	**la muchacha**	*lah moo-**chah**-chah*
husband	**el esposo**	*ehl ehs-**poh**-soh*
husband	**el marido**	*ehl mah-**ree**-doh*
wife	**la esposa**	*lah ehs-**poh**-sah*

Clothing

Clothing	**La ropa**	*lah **roh**-pah*
bathing suit	**el traje de baño**	*ehl **trah**-heh deh **bah**-nyoh*
bathrobe	**la bata**	*lah **bah**-tah*
belt	**el cinturón**	*ehl seen-too-**rohn***
blouse	**la blusa**	*lah **bloo**-sah*
boots	**las botas**	*lahs **boh**-tahs*
buckle	**la hebilla**	*lah **eh**-bee-yah*
button	**el botón**	*ehl boh-**tohn***
cap (baseball)	**la gorra**	*lah **goh**-rrah*
collar	**el cuello**	*ehl **kweh**-yoh*
dress	**el vestido**	*ehl vehs-**tee**-doh*
gloves	**los guantes**	*lohs **gwahn**-tehs*

Clothing (cntd.)

jacket	**la chaqueta**	*lah chah-**keh**-tah*
overcoat	**el abrigo**	*ehl ah-**bree**-goh*
pajamas	**los pijamas**	*lohs pee-**yah**-mahs*
panties	**las bragas**	*lahs **brah**-gahs*
pants	**los pantalones**	*lohs pahn-tah-**loh**-nehs*
raincoat	**el impermeable**	*ehl eem-pehr-meh-**ah**-bleh*
sandals	**las sandalias**	*lahs sahn-**dah**-leeahs*
scarf	**la bufanda**	*lah boo-**fahn**-dah*
shirt	**la camisa**	*lah kah-**mee**-sah*
shoes	**los zapatos**	*los sah-**pah**-tohs*
shorts	**los pantalones cortos**	*lohs pahn-tah-**loh**-nehs **kohr**-tohs*

Clothing (cntd.)

skirt	**la falda**	*lah **fahl**-dah*
socks	**los calcetines**	*lohs kahl-seh-**tee**-nehs*
sportcoat	**el saco**	*ehl **sah**-koh*
stockings	**las medias**	*lahs **meh**-dyahs*
suit	**el traje**	*ehl **trah**-heh*
sweater	**el suéter**	*ehl **sweh**-tehr*
sweatsuit	**la sudadera**	*lah soo-dah-**deh**-rah*
t-shirt	**la camiseta**	*lah kah-mee-**seh**-tah*
tennis shoes	**los tenis**	*lohs **teh**-nees*
tie	**la corbata**	*lah kohr-**bah**-tah*
underwear	**la ropa interior**	*lah **roh**-pah een-teh-**reeohr***
vest	**el chaleco**	*ehl chah-**leh**-koh*

Jewelry

The jewelry	**Las joyas**	*lahs **hoh**-yahs*
bracelet	**la pulsera**	*lah pool-**seh**-rah*
chain	**la cadena**	*lah kah-**deh**-nah*
diamonds	**los diamantes**	*lohs deeah-**mahn**-tehs*
earrings	**los aretes**	*lohs ah-**reh**-tehs*
gold	**el oro**	*ehl **oh**-roh*
necklace	**el collar**	*ehl **koh**-yahr*
pearls	**las perlas**	*lahs **pehr**-lahs*
ring	**el anillo**	*ehl ah-**nee**-yoh*
silver	**la plata**	*lah **plah**-tah*
watch	**el reloj**	*ehl reh-**lohh***

Breads, Grains & Cereals

The food	La comida	lah koh-**mee**-dah
bread	el pan	ehl pahn
bread (sweet)	el pan dulce	ehl pahn **dool**-seh
biscuit	el bizcocho	ehl bees-**koh**-choh
cereal	el cereal	ehl seh-reh-**ahl**
cornbread	el pan de maíz	ehl pahn deh mah-**ees**
crackers	las galletas	lahs gah-**yeh**-tahs
french bread	el pan francés	ehl pahn frahn-**sehs**
muffin	el panecillo	ehl pah-neh-**see**-yoh
toast	la tostada	lah tohs-**tah**-dah
oatmeal	la avena	lah ah-**veh**-nah

Vegetables

Vegetables	**Los vegetales**	*lohs veh-heh-**tah**-lehs*
asparagus	**el espárrago**	*ehl ehs-**pah**-rrah-goh*
beans	**los frijoles**	*lohs free-**hoh**-lehs*
beet	**la remolacha**	*lah reh-moh-**lah**-cha*
broccoli	**el brécol**	*ehl **breh**-kohl*
cabbage	**el repollo**	*ehl reh-**poh**-yoh*
carrot	**la zanahoria**	*lah sah-nah-**oh**-reeah*
cauliflower	**la coliflor**	*lah koh-lee-**flohr***
celery	**el apio**	*ehl **ah**-pyoh*
corn	**el maíz**	*ehl mah-**ees***
cucumber	**el pepino**	*ehl peh-**pee**-noh*
eggplant	**la berenjena**	*lah beh-rehn-**heh**-nah*

Vegetables (cntd.)

garlic	**el ajo**	*ehl **ah**-hoh*
green bean	**la judía verde**	*lah hoo-**dee**-ah **vehr**-deh*
lettuce	**la lechuga**	*lah leh-**choo**-gah*
mushroom	**el champiñón**	*ehl chahm-pee-**nyohn***
onion	**la cebolla**	*lah seh-**boh**-yah*
peas	**los guisantes**	*lohs gee-**sahn**-tehs*
potato	**la papa**	*lah **pah**-pah*
radish	**el rábano**	*ehl **rah**-bah-noh*
spinach	**la espinaca**	*lah ehs-pee-**nah**-kah*
squash	**la calabaza**	*lah kah-lah-**bah**-sah*
sweet potato	**el camote**	*ehl kah-**moh**-teh*
tomato	**el tomate**	*ehl toh-**mah**-teh*

Fish & Seafood

Seafood	**Los mariscos**	*lohs mah-**rees**-kohs*
clams	**las almejas**	*lahs ahl-**meh**-has*
crab	**el cangrejo**	*ehl kahn-**greh**-hoh*
fish	**el pescado**	*ehl pehs-**kah**-doh*
halibut	**el hálibut**	*ehl **ah**-lee-boot*
lobster	**la langosta**	*lah lahn-**gohs**-tah*
oysters	**la ostra**	*lah **ohs**-trah*
salmon	**el salmón**	*ehl sahl-**mohn***
shrimp	**los camarones**	*lohs kah-mah-**roh**-nehs*
squid	**el calamar**	*ehl kah-lah-**mahr***
trout	**la trucha**	*lah **troo**-chah*
tuna	**el atún**	*ehl ah-**toon***

Meat, Chicken & Pork

Meat	**La carne**	*lah **kahr**-neh*
...from beef	**...de vaca/de res**	*deh **vah**-kah /deh rehs*
...from lamb	**...de cordero**	*deh kohr-**deh**-roh*
...from pork	**...de cerdo**	*deh **sehr**-doh*
...from veal	**...de ternera**	*deh tehr-**neh**-rah*
bacon	**el tocino**	*ehl toh-**see**-noh*
chicken	**el pollo**	*ehl **poh**-yoh*
duck	**el pato**	*ehl **pah**-toh*
ham	**el jamón**	*ehl hah-**mohn***
liver	**el hígado**	*ehl **ee**-gah-doh*
sausage	**las salchichas**	*lahs sahl-**chee**-chahs*
turkey	**el pavo**	*ehl **pah**-voh*

Dairy Products

butter	**la mantequilla**	*lah mahn-teh-__kee__-yah*
cheese	**el queso**	*ehl __keh__-soh*
cottage cheese	**el requesón**	*ehl reh-keh-__sohn__*
cream cheese	**el queso de nata**	*ehl __keh__-soh deh __nah__-tah*
cream	**la crema**	*lah __kreh__-mah*
sour cream	**la crema agria**	*lah __kreh__-mah __ah__-gree-ah*
whipped cream	**la crema batida**	*lah __kreh__-mah bah-__tee__-dah*
eggs	**los huevos**	*lohs __hweh__-bohs*
margarine	**la margarina**	*lah mahr-gah-__ree__-nah*
omelette	**la tortilla**	*lah tohr-__tee__-yah*
milk	**la leche**	*lah __leh__-cheh*
yogurt	**el yogur**	*ehl ee-oh-__goohr__*

Ingredients & Condiments

broth	**el caldo**	*ehl **kahl**-doh*
cinnamon	**la canela**	*lah kah-**neh**-lah*
condiments	**los condimentos**	*lohs kohn-dee-**mehn**-tohs*
cornmeal	**la harina de maíz**	*lah ah-**ree**-nah deh mah-**ees***
flour	**la harina**	*lah ah-**ree**-nah*
garlic	**el ajo**	*ehl **ah**-hoh*
honey	**la miel**	*lah **myehl***
ingredients	**los ingredientes**	*lohs een-greh-**dyehn**-tehs*
jam/jelly	**la mermelada**	*lah mehr-meh-**lah**-dah*
mayonnaise	**la mayonesa**	*lah mah-yoh-**neh**-sah*
mint	**la menta**	*lah **mehn**-tah*
mustard	**la mostaza**	*lah mohs-**tah**-sah*

Ingredients & Condiments (cntd.)

nuts	**las nueces**	*lahs **nweh**-sehs*
olive oil	**el aceite de aceituna**	*ehl ah-**sehy**-teh deh ah-sehy-**too**-nah*
pepper	**la pimienta**	*lah pee-mee-**ehn**-tah*
salt	**la sal**	*lah sahl*
sauce	**la salsa**	*lah **sahl**-sah*
shortening	**la manteca**	*lah mahn-**teh**-kah*
spices	**las especias**	*lahs ehs-**peh**-syahs*
sugar	**el azúcar**	*ehl ah-**soo**-kahr*
syrup	**el jarabe**	*ehl hah-**rah**-beh*
vanilla	**la vainilla**	*lah vahee-**nee**-yah*
vinegar	**el vinagre**	*ehl vee-**nah**-greh*

Containers

bag	**la bolsa**	*lah **bohl**-sah*
basket	**la canasta**	*lah kah-**nahs**-tah*
bottle	**la botella**	*lah boh-**teh**-yah*
box	**la caja**	*lah **kah**-hah*
bucket	**el balde**	*ehl **bahl**-deh*
can	**la lata**	*lah **lah**-tah*
carton	**el cartón**	*ehl kahr-**tohn***
jar	**el jarro**	*ehl **hah**-rroh*
package	**el paquete**	*ehl pah-**keh**-teh*
paper	**el papel**	*ehl pah-**pehl***
plastic	**el plástico**	*ehl **plahs**-tee-koh*

The House

The house	**La casa**	*lah **kah**-sah*
attic	**el desván**	*ehl dehs-**vahn***
basement	**el sótano**	*ehl **soh**-tah-noh*
bathroom	**el baño**	*ehl **bah**-nyoh*
bedroom	**el dormitorio**	*ehl dohr-mee-**toh**-reeoh*
dining room	**el comedor**	*ehl koh-meh-**dohr***
garage	**el garaje**	*ehl gah-**rah**-heh*
kitchen	**la cocina**	*lah koh-**see**-nah*
laundry	**la lavandería**	*lah lah-vahn-deh-**ree**-ah*
library	**la biblioteca**	*lah bee-blee-oh-**teh**-kah*
living room	**la sala de estar**	*lah **sah**-lah deh ehs-**tahr***

Inside & Outside

ceiling	**el techo**	*ehl **teh**-choh*
closet	**el armario**	*ehl ahr-**mah**-reeoh*
door	**la puerta**	*lah **pwehr**-tah*
fireplace	**la chimenea**	*lah chee-meh-**neh**-ah*
floor (room)	**el suelo**	*ehl **sweh**-loh*
light	**la luz**	*lah loos*
porch	**el porche**	*ehl **pohr**-cheh*
roof	**el techo**	*ehl **teh**-cho*
stairs	**la escalera**	*lah ehs-kah-**leh**-rah*
terrace	**la terraza**	*lah teh-**rrah**-sah*
wall	**la pared**	*lah pah-**rehd***
window	**la ventana**	*lah vehn-**tah**-nah*

In the Kitchen

In the kitchen	**En la cocina**	*ehn lah koh-see-nah*
the cook	**el cocinero**	*ehl koh-see-neh-roh*
apron	**el delantal**	*ehl deh-lahn-tahl*
coffee pot	**la cafetera**	*lah kah-feh-teh-rah*
dishes	**los platos**	*lohs plah-tohs*
pan	**el sartén**	*ehl sahr-tehn*
pot	**la olla**	*lah oh-yah*
pitcher	**el cántaro**	*ehl kahn-tah-roh*
silverware	**los cubiertos**	*lohs koo-byehr-tohs*
saucepan	**la cacerola**	*lah kah-seh-roh-lah*
tea kettle	**la tetera**	*lah teh-teh-rah*
tray	**la bandeja**	*lah bahn-deh-hah*

Appliances

blender	**la licuadora**	*lah lee-kwah-**doh**-rah*
can opener	**el abrelatas**	*ehl ah-breh-**lah**-tahs*
dishwasher	**el lavaplatos**	*ehl lah-vah-**plah**-tohs*
dryer	**la secadora**	*lah seh-kah-**dohr**-ah*
freezer	**el congelador**	*ehl kohn-heh-lah-**dohr***
mixer	**la batidora**	*lah bah-tee-**doh**-rah*
oven	**el horno**	*ehl **ohr**-noh*
refrigerator	**la nevera**	*lah neh-**veh**-rah*
stove	**la cocina**	*lah koh-**see**-nah*
vacuum cleaner	**la aspiradora**	*lah ahs-pee-rah-**doh**-rah*
washing machine	**la lavadora**	*lah lah-vah-**doh**-rah*

The Laundry

The laundry	**La lavandería**	*lah lah-vahn-deh-**ree**-ah*
broom	**la escoba**	*lah ehs-**koh**-bah*
detergent	**el detergente**	*ehl deh-tehr-**hehn**-teh*
dirty clothes	**la ropa sucia**	*lah **roh**-pah **soo**-syah*
hangers	**los ganchos**	*lohs **gahn**-chohs*
iron	**la plancha**	*lah **plahn**-chah*
ironing board	**la mesa de planchar**	*lah **meh**-sah deh plahn-**chahr***
mop	**el trapeador**	*ehl trah-peh-ah-**dohr***
sponge	**la esponja**	*lah ehs-**pohn**-hah*
stain	**la mancha**	*lah-**mahn**-chah*
starch	**el almidón**	*ehl ahl-mee-**dohn***

Patio & Garden

The patio	**El patio**	*ehl **pah**-tyoh*
butterfly	**la mariposa**	*lah mah-ree-**poh**-sah*
flowers	**las flores**	*lahs **floh**-rehs*
fly	**la mosca**	*lah **mohs**-kah*
fly swatter	**el matamoscas**	*ehl mah-tah-**mohs**-kahs*
garden	**el jardín**	*ehl hahr-**deen***
grass	**el césped**	*ehl **sehs**-pehd*
insects	**los insectos**	*lohs een-**sehk**-tohs*
lawn mower	**la cortadora de grama**	*lah kohr-tah-**doo**-rah deh **grah**-mah*
pool	**la piscina**	*lah pee-**see**-nah*
shade	**la sombra**	*lah **sohm**-brah*
tree	**el árbol**	*ehl **ahr**-bohl*

Tools & Materials

ax	**el hacha**	*ehl **ah**-chah*
cord (electric)	**el cordón eléctrico**	*ehl kohr-**dohn** eh-**lehk**-tree-koh*
drill	**el taladro**	*ehl tah-**lah**-droh*
flashlight	**la linterna eléctrica**	*lah leen-**tehr**-nah eh-**lehk**-tree-kah*
glue	**el pegamento**	*ehl peh-gah-**mehn**-toh*
hammer	**el martillo**	*ehl mahr-**tee**-yoh*
hoe	**el azadón**	*ehl ah-sah-**dohn***
hose	**la manguera**	*lah mahn-**geh**-rah*
jack	**el gato**	*ehl **gah**-toh*
ladder	**la escalera**	*lah ehs-kah-**leh**-rah*
level	**el nivel**	*ehl nee-**vehl***

Tools & Materials (cntd.)

nails	**los clavos**	*lohs **klah**-vohs*
paint	**la pintura**	*lah peen-**too**-rah*
pliers	**las pinzas**	*lahs **peen**-sahs*
rake	**el rastrillo**	*ehl rahs-**tree**-yoh*
saw	**el serrucho**	*ehl seh-**rroo**-choh*
screw	**el tornillo**	*ehl tohr-**nee**-yoh*
screwdriver	**el destornillador**	*ehl dehs-tohr-nee-yah-**dohr***
shovel	**la pala**	*lah **pah**-lah*
tape measure	**la cinta para medir**	*lah **seen**-tah **pah**-rah meh-**deer***
tools	**las herramientas**	*lahs eh-rrah-**myehn**-tahs*
wheelbarrow	**la carretilla**	*lah kah-rreh-**tee**-yah*
wrench	**la llave**	*lah **yah**-veh*

Trips & Travel

airplane	**el avión**	*ehl ah-vyohn*
airport	**el aeropuerto**	*ehl ah-eh-roh-pwehr-toh*
aisle	**el pasillo**	*ehl pah-see-yoh*
arrival	**la llegada**	*lah yeh-gah-dah*
baggage claim	**la contraseña de equipaje**	*lah kohn-trah-seh-nyah deh eh-kee-pah-heh*
customs	**la aduana**	*lah ah-dwah-nah*
departure	**la partida**	*lah pahr-tee-dah*
destination	**el destino**	*ehl dehs-tee-noh*
entrance	**la entrada**	*lah ehn-trah-dah*
flight	**el vuelo**	*ehl vweh-loh*
gate	**la puerta**	*lah pwehr-tah*

Trips & Travel

luggage	**el equipaje**	*ehl eh-kee-**pah**-heh*
passengers	**los pasajeros**	*lohs pah-sah-**heh**-rohs*
passport	**el pasaporte**	*ehl pah-sah-**pohr**-teh*
pilot	**el piloto**	*ehl pee-**loh**-toh*
porter	**el mozo de equipaje**	*ehl **moh**-soh deh eh-kee-**pah**-heh*
runway	**la pista**	*lah **pees**-tah*
seat belt	**el cinturón de seguridad**	*ehl seen-too-**rohn** deh seh-goo-ree-**dahd***
suitcase	**la maleta**	*lah mah-**leh**-tah*
ticket counter	**el mostrador de boletos**	*ehl mohs-trah-**dohr** deh boh-**leh**-tohs*
tickets	**los boletos**	*lohs boh-**leh**-tohs*

The Restaurant

appetizers	**los aperitivos**	*lohs ah-peh-ree-tee-vohs*
bar	**el bar**	*ehl bahr*
breakfast	**el desayuno**	*ehl deh-sah-yoo-noh*
check	**la cuenta**	*lah kwehn-tah*
cook	**el cocinero**	*ehl koh-see-neh-roh*
dinner	**la cena**	*lah seh-nah*
lunch	**el almuerzo**	*ehl ahl-mwehr-soh*
menu	**el menú**	*ehl meh-noo*
reservation	**la reservación**	*lah reh-sehr-vah-syon*
snack/tea	**la merienda**	*lah meh-reeehn-dah*
tip	**la propina**	*lah proh-pee-nah*
waiter	**el camarero**	*ehl kah-mah-reh-roh*

Who's Calling

Hello!	¡Aló!, ¡Oiga!
Hello!	¡Diga!, ¡Bueno!
Who's calling?	¿De parte de quién?, ¿Quién habla?
I would like to speak to...	Quisiera hablar con...
Can I speak with...?	¿Puedo hablar con...?
Is Maria in?	¿Está María?
When will she return?	¿Cuándo va a regresar?
Don't hang up!	¡No cuelgue!
May I leave a message?	¿Puedo dejar un recado?
I'll call back...	Volveré a llamar...
Call me back...	Vuelva a llamarme...

The Stores

The stores	**Las tiendas**	*lahs **tyehn**-dahs*
bakery	**la pandadería**	*lah pah-nah-deh-**ree**-ah*
beauty shop	**la peluquería**	*lah peh-loo-keh-**ree**-ah*
bookstore	**la librería**	*lah lee-breh-**ree**-ah*
candy store	**la confitería**	*lah kohn-fee-teh-**ree**-ah*
clothing store	**el almacén**	*ehl ahl-mah-**sehn***
dry cleaner	**la tienda de lavado en seco**	*lah **tyehn**-dah deh lah-**bah**-doh ehn **seh**-koh*
fish store	**la pescadería**	*lah pehs-kah-deh-**ree**-ah*
florist	**la florería**	*lah floh-reh-**ree**-ah*
furniture store	**la tienda de muebles**	*lah **teeehn**-dah deh **mweh**-blehs*

The Stores (cntd.)

grocery store	**la tienda de comestibles**	*lah **tyehn**-dah de koh-mehs-**tee**-blehs*
jewelry store	**la joyería**	*lah hoh-yeh-**ree**-ah*
laundromat	**la lavandería**	*lah lah-vahn-deh-**ree**-ah*
meat market	**la carnicería**	*lah kahr-nee-seh-**ree**-ah*
newsstand	**el quiosco**	*ehl **kee**-oh-skoh*
pastry shop	**la pastelería**	*lah pah-steh-leh-**ree**-ah*
pharmacy	**la farmacia**	*lah fahr-**mah**-syah*
restaurant	**el restaurante**	*ehl rehs-tahw-**rahn**-teh*
saloon (beer)	**la cervecería**	*lah sehr-beh-seh-**ree**-ah*
shoe store	**la zapatería**	*lah sah-pah-teh-**ree**-ah*
toy store	**la juguetería**	*lah hoo-geh-teh-**ree**-ah*

In the Hotel

Where is..?	**¿Dónde está...?**	*dohn-deh ehs-tah*
the bellhop	**el botones**	*ehl boh-toh-nehs*
the concierge	**el conserje**	*ehl kohn-sehr-heh*
the doorman	**el portero**	*ehl pohr-teh-roh*
the elevator	**el ascensor**	*ehl ah-sehn-sohr*
the floor*	**el piso**	*ehl pee-soh*
the key	**la llave**	*lah yah-veh*
the maid	**la criada**	*lah kree-ah-dah*
the manager	**el gerente**	*ehl heh-rehn-teh*
the pool	**la piscina**	*lah pee-see-nah*

* The word *piso* (*floor*) refers to floors above the ground.
The ground floor is called *la planta baja* (*the lower floor*).

In the Hotel (cntd.)

I need...	**Necesito...**	*neh-seh-**see**-toh*
a blanket	**una manta**	*oo-nah **mahn**-tah*
a pillow	**una almohada**	*oo-nah ahl-moh-**ah**-dah*
a room	**una habitación**	*oo-nah ah-bee-tah-**syohn***
...single	**...con una cama**	*kohn oo-nah **kah**-mah*
...double	**...con dos camas**	*kohn dohs **kah**-mahs*
a sheet	**una sábana**	*oo-nah **sah**-bah-nah*
a shower	**una ducha**	*oo-nah **doo**-chah*
more ice	**más hielo**	*mahs **yeh**-loh*
more soap	**más jabón**	*mahs **hah**-bohn*
more towels	**más toallas**	*mahs toh-**ah**-yahs*
toilet paper	**papel higiénico**	*pah-**pehl** ee-**hyeh**-nee-koh*

In the Classroom

The classroom	**La aula**	*lah **ah**-oo-lah*
books	**los libros**	*lohs **lee**-brohs*
chalk	**la tiza**	*lah **tee**-sah*
chalkboard	**la pizarra**	*lah pee-**sah**-rrah*
crayons	**el creyón**	*ehl kreh-**yohn***
homework	**la tarea**	*lah tah-**reh**-ah*
map	**el mapa**	*ehl **mah**-pah*
notebook	**el cuaderno**	*ehl kwah-**dehr**-noh*
problems	**los problemas**	*lohs proh-**bleh**-mahs*
pupil's desk	**el pupitre**	*ehl poo-**pee**-treh*
student	**el estudiante**	*ehl ehs-too-**dyahn**-teh*
teacher	**el maestro**	*ehl **mah**-ehs-troh*

Games & Toys

Toys	**Los jugetes**	*lohs hoo-**geh**-tehs*
cards	**los naipes**	*lohs **nahee**-pehs*
checkers	**el juego de damas**	*ehl **hweh**-goh deh **dah**-mahs*
chess	**el ajedrez**	*ehl ah-**heh**-drehs*
doll	**la muñeca**	*lah moo-**nyeh**-kah*
games	**los juegos**	*lohs **hweh**-gohs*
kite	**la cometa**	*lah koh-**meh**-tah*
marbles	**las canicas**	*lahs kah-**nee**-kahs*
puzzle	**el rompecabezas**	*ehl rohm-peh-kah-**beh**-sahs*
seesaw	**el sube y baja**	*ehl **soo**-beh ee **bah**-hah*
slide	**el tobagán**	*ehl toh-bah-**gahn***
swing	**el columpio**	*ehl koh-**loom**-pyoh*

Post Office

Post office	**El correo**	*ehl koh-rreh-oh*
address	**la dirección**	*lah dee-rehk-syohn*
addressee	**el destinatario**	*ehl dehs-tee-nah-tah-ree-ho*
airmail	**el correo aéreo**	*ehl koh-rreh-oh ah-eh-reh-oh*
certified	**certificada**	*sehr-tee-fee-kah-dah*
envelope	**el sobre**	*ehl soh-breh*
insured	**asegurada**	ah-*seh-goo-rah-dah*
label	**la etiqueta**	*lah eh-tee-keh-tah*
letter	**la carta**	*lah kahr-tah*
mail	**el correo**	*ehl koh-rreh-oh*
mail box	**el buzón**	*ehl boo-sohn*
money order	**el giro postal**	*ehl hee-roh pohs-tahl*

Post Office (cntd.)

package	**el paquete**	*ehl pah-**keh**-teh*
postage	**el franqueo**	*ehl frahn-**keh**-oh*
postcard	**la tarjeta postal**	*lah tahr-**heh**-tah pohs-**tahl***
postmark	**el matasellos**	*ehl mah-tah-**seh**-yohs*
rate	**la tarifa**	*lah tah-**ree**-fah*
scale	**la balanza**	*lah bah-**lahn**-sah*
sender	**el remitente**	*ehl reh-mee-**tehn**-teh*
stamp	**el sello**	*ehl **seh**-yoh*
string	**la cuerda**	*lah **kwehr**-dah*
telegram	**el telegrama**	*ehl teh-leh-**grah**-mah*
tape	**la cinta**	*lah **seen**-tah*
zip code	**el código postal**	*ehl **koh**-dee-goh pohs-**tahl***

Directions & Locations

over there	**allá**	*ah-**yah***
straight ahead	**adelante**	*ah-deh-**lahn**-teh*
anywhere	**cualquier parte**	*kwahl-**kyehr pahr**-teh*
everywhere	**por todas partes**	*pohr **toh**-dahs **pahr**-tehs*
nowhere	**por ningún lado**	*pohr neen-**goon lah**-doh*
somewhere	**por algún lugar**	*pohr ahl-**goon** loo-**gahr***
to the east	**al este**	*ahl **ehs**-teh*
to the west	**al oeste**	*ahl oh-**ehs**-teh*
to the north	**al norte**	*ahl **nohr**-teh*
to the south	**al sur**	*ahl soor*
to the right	**a la derecha**	*ah lah deh-**reh**-chah*
to the left	**a la izquierda**	*a lah ees-**kyehr**-dah*

Points of Interest

aquarium	**el acuario**	jungle	**la jungla**
beach	**la playa**	museum	**el museo**
castle	**el castillo**	ocean	**el mar**
cathedral	**la catedral**	palace	**el palacio**
church	**la iglesia**	park	**el parque**
circus	**el circo**	ruins	**las ruinas**
city	**la ciudad**	stadium	**el estadio**
concert	**el concierto**	square	**la plaza**
country	**el campo**	statue	**la estatua**
disco	**la discoteca**	the king	**el rey**
fair	**la feria**	the queen	**la reina**
fountain	**la fuente**	theatre	**el teatro**

Survival Phrases

Can you help me?	**¿Puede ayudarme?**
How do you say it?	**¿Cómo se dice?**
How do you spell it?	**¿Cómo se deletrea?**
I don't understand.	**No comprendo.**
Do you understand?	**¿Comprende?**
Speak slower.	**Hable más despacio.**
Where is the bathroom?	**¿Dónde está el baño?**
Where are you from?	**¿De dónde eres?**
Excuse me!	**¡Perdón! (¡Disculpe!)**
May I come in?	**¿Puedo entrar?**
I need to find...	**Necesito encontrar...**
Help!	**¡Socorro!**

Common Phrases!

Good for you!	¡Así se hace!
Really?	¿De veras?
I think so.	Creo que sí.
I hope so.	Ojalá.
I'm coming.	Ya vengo.
I'm going.	Ya me voy.
He/she has gone (left).	Ya se fue.
Of course.	Como no.
Sure.	Claro.
Just a minute.	Un momento.
As a matter of fact...	En realidad...
Finally... (At last...)	Por fin... (Por último...)

Common Phrases! (cntd.)

More or less.	**Más o menos.**
Maybe.	**Quizás.**
As usual.	**Como de costumbre.**
From today on...	**A partir de hoy...**
Me too.	**Yo también.**
Me neither.	**Yo tampoco.**
I'm very sorry.	**Lo siento mucho.**
In my opinion...	**En mi opinión...**
It's a deal!	**¡Trato hecho!**
It's almost time.	**Falta poco.**
Above all...	**Sobre todo...**
It seems to me that...	**Me parece que...**

¿Dónde?

¿Dónde está...?	Where is...?
¿Dónde están...?	Where are...?
¿Dónde estoy?	Where am I?
¿Dónde estás?	Where are you? (informal)
¿Dónde vive?	Where do you live?
¿Dónde trabaja?	Where do you work?
¿Dónde quiere comer?	Where do you want to eat?
¿De dónde es?	Where are you from?
¿Adónde va?	Where are you going?
¿Adónde quiere ir?	Where do you want to go?

¿Cuándo?

¿Cuándo sale?	When does it leave?
¿Cuándo llega?	When does it arrive?
¿Cuándo empieza?	When does it start?
¿Cuándo termina?	When does it finish?
¿Cuándo regresa?	When does it return?
¿Cuándo pasó esto?	When did this happen?
¿Cuándo quiere comer?	When do you want to eat?
¿Cuándo estará listo?	When will it be ready?
¿Cuándo nació?	When were you born?
¿Cuándo es su cumpleaños?	When is your birthday?
¿Para cuándo lo quiere?	When do you want it?

¿Cómo?

¿Cómo?	What?
¿Cómo se llama?	What is your name?
¿Cómo está?	How are you?
¿Cómo se dice...?	How do you say...?
¿Cómo le va?	How's it going?
¿Cómo se escribe?	How do you write it?
¿Cómo se deletrea?	How do you spell it?
¿Cómo lo sabe?	How do you know?
¿Cómo quiere pagar?	How do you want to pay?
Yo no sé cómo.	I don't know how.
¡Como has crecido!	You've really grown! (informal)
¡Como no!	But of course!

¿Qué?

¿Qué hora es (son)?	What time is it?
¿Qué tal?	How are things?
¿Qué hubo?	What's up?
¿Qué le parece...?	How do you like...?
¿Qué sé yo?	How should I know?
¿Qué es esto?	What's this?
¿Qué significa?	What does it mean?
¿Qué dijo?	What did you say?
¿Qué haces?	What are you doing?
¿Qué hay de malo con eso?	What's wrong with that?
¿Qué hay de nuevo?	What's new?
¡Qué lástima!	What a shame! / Too bad!

¿Cuál?

¿Cuál?	Which one?
¿Cuáles?	Which ones?
¿Cuál es su nombre?	What is your name?
¿Cuál es su apellido?	What is your last name?
¿Cuál es su dirección?	What is your address?
¿Cuál es su número de teléfono?	What is your telephone number?
¿Cuál es suyo?	Which one is yours?
¿Cuál le gusta?	Which one do you like?
¿Cuál es?	Which (one) is it?
¿Cuál es la fecha hoy?	What is the date today?

¿Cuánto?

¿Cuántos años tiene?	How old are you?
¿Cuánto cuesta?	How much does it cost?
¿Cuánto es?	How much is it?
¿Cuánto pagó?	How much did you pay?
¿Cuánto vale?	How much is it worth?
¿Por cuánto tiempo?	For how long?
¿Cuántos quiere?	How many do you want?
¿A cuánto(s) estamos?	What is the date?
¿Cuántos tiene?	How many do you have?
¿Cuánto le debo?	How much do I owe you?
¿Cuántas veces?	How many times?

Personal "A"

Spanish requires the preposition *a* before a direct object that refers to a person or pet. This personal *a* does not translate into English.

*Necesito llamar **a** mi tía. (I need to call my aunt.)*
*Visité **a** Juan. (I visited Juan.)*
*Ayudo **a** mis amigos. (I help my friends.)*

This personal *a* is not used with the verb tener.

Tengo dos hermanas. (I have two sisters.)

Verbs that are frequently followed by a personal *a* include:

ayudar	*to help*	**invitar**	*to invite*
buscar	*to look for*	**llamar**	*to call*
cuidar	*to care for*	**mirar**	*to watch*
esperar	*to wait for*	**preguntar**	*to ask*

This & That

Use the chart below to choose the correct form of *this*, *that*, *these* and *those*. Notice how the demonstrative adjective changes depending on the gender and proximity of the noun to which it refers.

Meaning	Masculine	Feminine
this (here)	*este* libro	*esta* mesa
these (here)	*estos* libros	*estas* mesas
that (near listener)	*ese* libro	*esa* mesa
those (near listener)	*esos* libros	*esas* mesas
that (over there)	*aquel* libro	*aquella* mesa
those (over there)	*aquellos* libros	*aquellas* mesas

This & That (cntd.)

To express *this one*, *that one*, *these* or *those* without specifically mention-
ing the object, use the demonstrative pronouns in the chart below. They are
just like demonstrative pronouns (pg. 236) only they have accents.

Meaning	Masculine	Feminine	Neuter
this one (here)	*éste*	*ésta*	*esto*
these (here)	*éstos*	*éstas*	
that one (near listener)	*ése*	*ésa*	*eso*
those (near listener)	*ésos*	*ésas*	
that one (over there)	*aquél*	*aquélla*	*aquello*
those (over there)	*aquéllos*	*aquéllas*	

Use the demonstrative pronouns *esto*, *eso* and *aquello* when you have no
specific object in mind. These *neuter* pronouns always end in *-o*.

Common Measurements

Conversion Table

1 millimeter	=	.0400 inches	1 inch	=	2.5400 centimeters

1 millimeter = .0400 inches   1 inch = 2.5400 centimeters

1 centimeter = .3940 inches   1 foot = 30.4800 centimeters

1 meter = 39.3700 inches   1 yard = 91.4400 centimeters

1 kilometer = 3,281.5 feet   1 mile = 1.6090 kilometers

1 kilometer = .621 miles

Metric Weights & Measures

1 liter = 1.057 quarts   1 ounce = 28.3500 grams

1 liter = .264 gallon   1 pound = 0.4540 kilograms

3.785 liters = 1 gallon

1 gram = .035 ounces

Inches → centimeters, multiply by 2.54

Centimeters → inches, multiply by .394